GOLF PUTTING CHARTS

\-   Concepts to help you putt more accurately

James C. Gerdeen

ISBN-10: 1985750589
ISBN-13: 978-1985750586

PREFACE

The details of this analysis were copyrighted in a paper in 2012, "Golfpath © - Predicting The Path Of Putting A Golf Ball On Sloping Greens". Then in 2017 more analyses and more results were published in a book, **Golf Ball Putting Analytics.** Also see www.Golfpath.net.

In this present book some of the significant results are presented in charts to help golfers improve their putting strokes on sloping greens. It is assumed that the greens have constant slope and the resistance is uniform. Actual green surfaces may vary. Never the less the basic concepts and insights presented here should help the golfer putt with more accuracy overall.

DEDICATION

This book is dedicated to Prof. Thomas Kane of Stanford University who taught this author how to understand dynamics and its applications.

Many thanks to my wife Wanda for graciously allowing me time to work on golf analysis and on this book for the past few years.

James C. Gerdeen, Consulting Engineer, Professor Emeritus University of Colorado at Denver, Distinguished Professor Michigan Technological University

CONTENTS

NOMENCLATURE

Vo   Initial putting velocity, feet per second, (fps)

X,Y Reference axes for charts, units in feet, (ft)

 X   Horizontal axis

Y   Vertical axis (axis toward hole when putting)

Xr, Yr   Values when ball comes to rest after putting

Yh Distance to the hole

Xh Target value, amount of offset from hole

ψ (psi)   Angle of the Fall Line, degrees

φ_o (phi) Angle of Target line

1 PUTTING MASTER CHART

The **Putting Master Chart** can be used for putting up hill or down hill for combined resistance from green roughness and gravity. When putting up hill the resistance of the green and the force of gravity both reduce the velocity. The effects add together. When putting down hill the resistance of the green is assumed greater than the gravity effect.

Insight: Really I don't need to know the value of the resistance or the degree of slope. All I need to know is where my ball comes to rest after a practice stroke.

Let Xr be that distance where the ball comes to rest.
Let Vor be the initial practice velocity.
Let Xh be the distance to the hole.

Then the master chart shows what initial velocity Voh is needed to reach the hole.

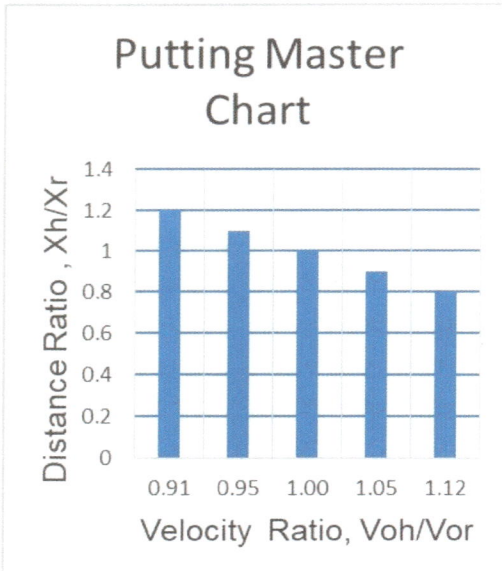

Putting Master Chart

The values in the chart are calculated from the equation
$$Vh^2/Vo^2 = Xh/Xr)$$
The examples below will illustrate how this works.

Example A. **Putting Up Hill**

This chart can be used for putting up hill for combined resistance from green roughness and gravity.

Assume the hole is at Xh = 10 ft and assume the practice putt goes 8 ft with a velocity of 6 fps. From the master chart we see we need to increase the velocity by about 10% or by 1.12 * 6 or 6.7 fps to reach hole at 10ft. (For Xh/Xr = 10/8, Voh/Vor = 1.12)

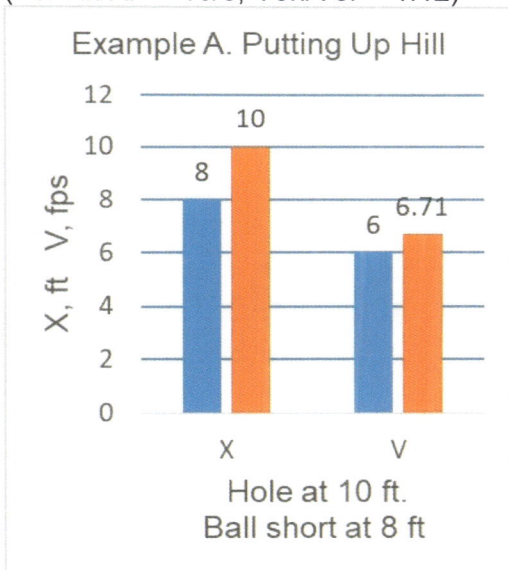

Example A. Putting Up Hill

Hole at 10 ft.
Ball short at 8 ft

You may not know the velocity of your stroke. Ok then interpret it this way: Increase the force of your stroke by about 10%.

Example B.

 This chart can be used for putting down hill for combined resistance from green roughness and gravity. When putting down hill the resistance of green is assumed greater than gravity effect.

 Again assume the hole is at Xh = 10 ft. Assume the practice putt goes 12 ft with velocity of 6 fps. For Xh/Xr = 12/10 we find from the master chart that we need to decrease the velocity to about 90% or to 0.91 * 6 or to 5.48 fps to reach hole at 10ft.

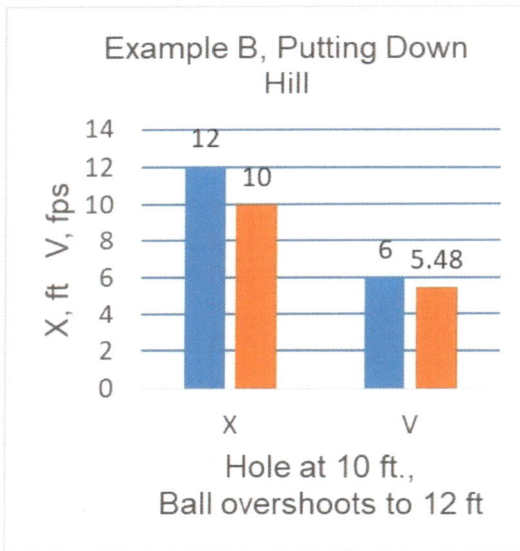

Example B, Putting Down Hill

Hole at 10 ft.,
Ball overshoots to 12 ft

2 PUTTING ACROSS A SLOPE

 The figure below shows a slope (Fall Line) to the left. The hole is located at a distance Yh. The target distance is Xh for aiming the putt. The angle of the line and the initial putting velocity (speed) Vo depend upon the slope and rolling resistance.

 To determine the break you take a practice putt or you

remember the break from your prievious round or you observe a putt by the previous golfer.

Example A
 Assume the Slope is 2% down to the left on a fast green. We try an initial velocity of 6 fps with our target at xh = 1 ft. for a hole at 10 ft.on a fast green

Result:
We miss to the right, but close. We may be satisfied with that since we have a short putt remaining.

Next we try to increase the velocity to see what happens.

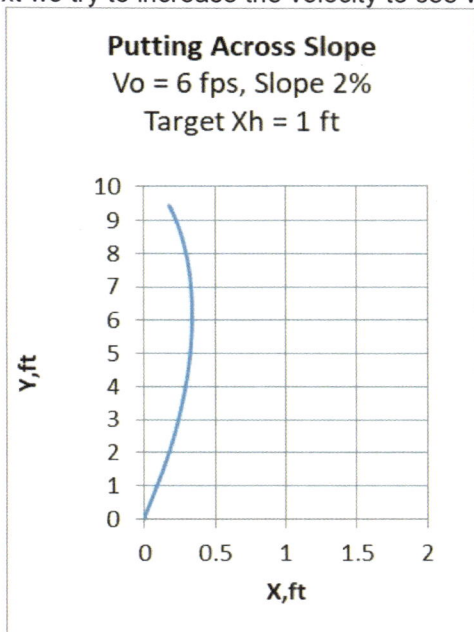

**Putting Across Slope
Vo = 6 fps, Slope 2%
Target Xh = 1 ft**

Y,ft

X,ft

We should not have to increase the velocity by very much. From the master chart equation we calculate Vo = 6* sqrt(10/9.5) = 6.16 fps. The Golfpath sofware gives the result below.

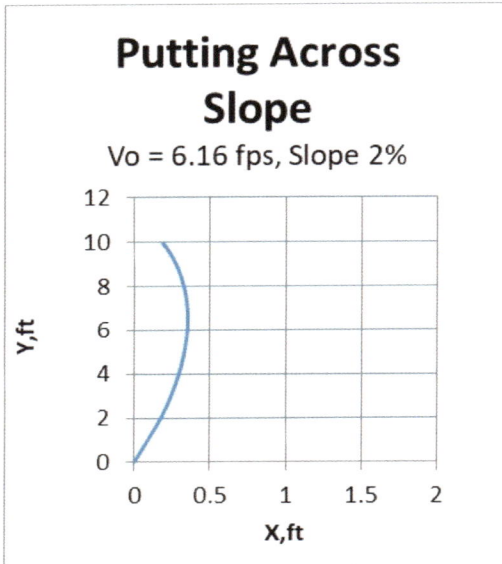

Putting Across Slope

Vo = 6.16 fps, Slope 2%

We find we reached 10 ft alright but we miss the hole to the right. Maybe we should hit the ball a little harder.

Example B .
So we try a larger velocity of 7 fps. The conditions are the same as Example A with a slope 2% down to the left, an Initial and a target at xh = 1 ft. on a fast green.

Result:
We still miss to the right.

Putting Across Slope
Vo = 7 fps, Slope 2%
Target Xh = 1 ft

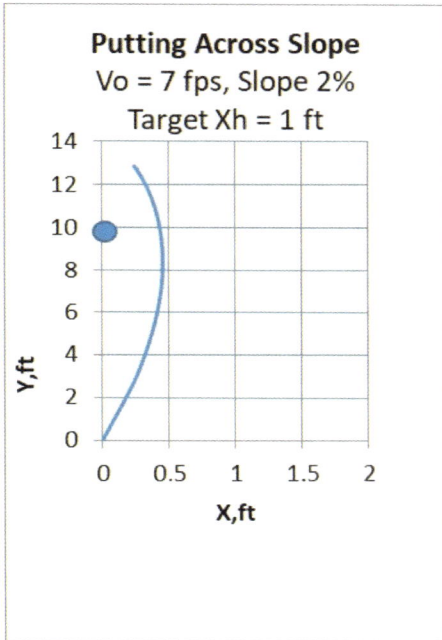

This shows we need to reduce target angle. Result is on the next chart.

Example C

The previous chart showed that increasing velocity for Xh = 1 ft missed the hole to the right. If we decrease target we have a chance to hit the hole.

Result:

We reduce the target to xh = 0.5 ft. Using the GOLFPATH software we can show that an initial velocity of 7.2 fps will give us a path to the hole at 10 ft
If we miss slightly the ball will come to rest 4 ft past the hole.

Putting Across Slope
Vo = 7.2 Fps, Slope 2%
Xh = 0.5 Ft

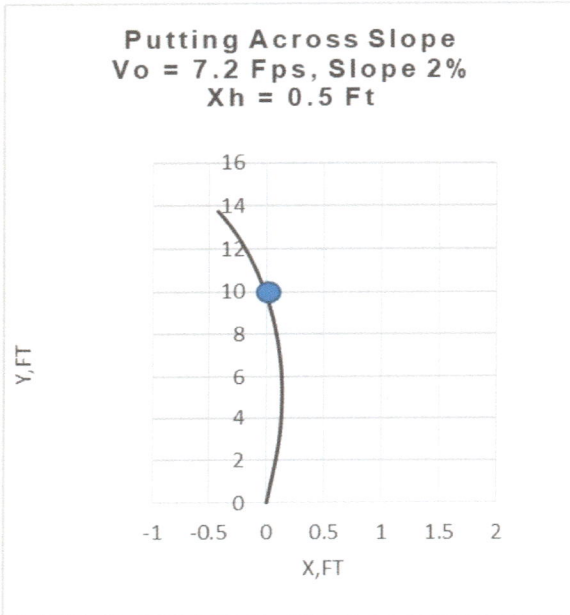

Similarity of Paths

From the previous examples we note that if the ball ends up to the right of the hole and if we increase the velocity then the ball ends up still right of the hole.

Insight: There is something basic going on.
As shown in the book **GOLF BALL PUTTING ANALYTICS,** the putting paths are similar for the same target line, constant slope and constant resistance. See the chart below.

Similarity of Paths

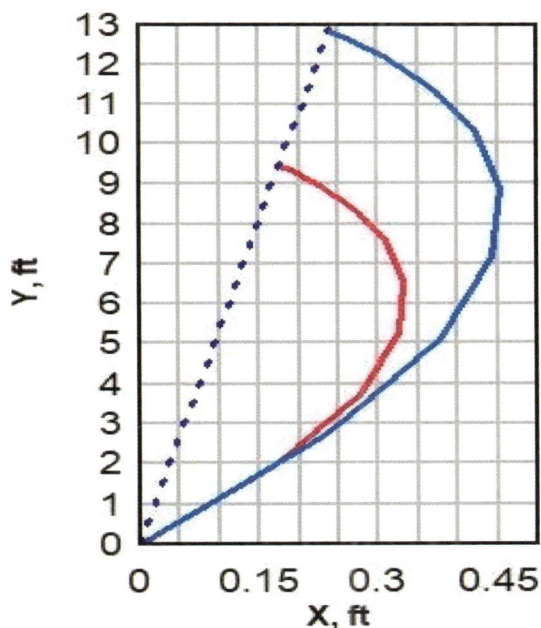

From the above curves we see that the ball reaches Y = 10 ft at a value of x about 0.2 ft. for Vo = 6 fps. So if we change our target to Xh = 1.0- .2 = 0.8 ft, what happens? Result is below.

Putting Across Slope

Vo = 6 fps, Slope 2%, xh = 0.8 ft

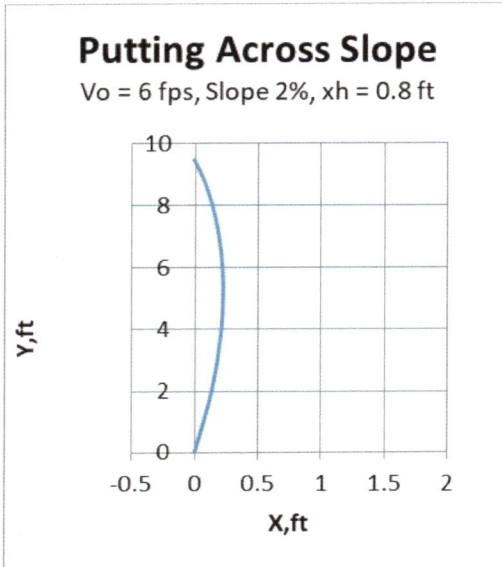

What have we learned? If ball misses to right we can reduce target X value by that amount and come nearer to the hole.

Putting Across a Greater Slope

Next we consider putting across a greater slope at different target angles.

Assume the Fall Line is to the left on a fast green. Let Vo = 6 fps
Assume a 2.5 degree slope (4.4%). Results are shown below.
(Note: In these charts (and others) the X and Y axes are not to the same scale in order to better see the difference

in the curves.)

PATH DEPENDENCE ON PUTTING ANGLE

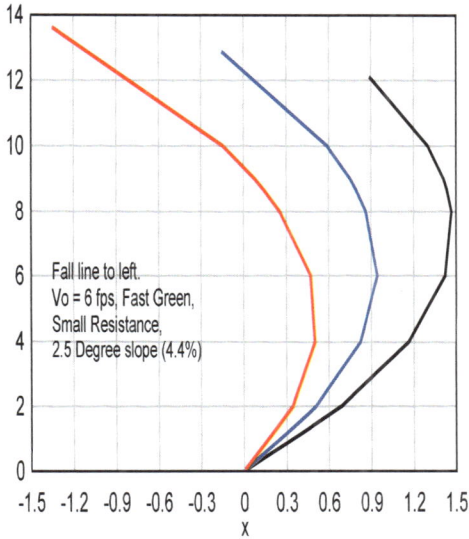

Fall line to left.
Vo = 6 fps, Fast Green,
Small Resistance,
2.5 Degree slope (4.4%)

Runaway Values of Slope

When one putts downhill there is a chance the ball will more easily run away run away. This can happen with zero velocity when gravity overcomes the resistance from the green. The table below gives critical values of slope when this occurs, i.e. when the ball refuses to stay at rest on the green.

Critical Values of Slope for Run Away

Green	Stimpmeter Reading, ft (Vo = 6 fps)	Angle,degees	Slope %
Fast	18	2.49	4.4
Fast	12	3.74	6.5
Fast	10.5	4.23	7.4
Medium	6.5	6.90	12.1
Slow	4.5	9.96	17.6

3 EFFECT OF SLOPE DIRECTION

One may ask, what is the effect if the slope has a different direction? In the figure below the slope direction or Fall Line orientation is defined by the angle ψ (psi) from the X axis.

Several examples will be considered. In all cases the following conditions will be assumed:

A slope of 2% to the left, a Hole at Yh = 10 ft., a target of Xh = 1 ft. , a Stimpmeter reading of 9.5 ft (fast green or small resistance), and an initial putt velocity of 6 ft/sec (fps).

Results are taken from Chapter 5 in the book, **Golf Ball**

Putting Analytics.

First for reference assume the Fall Line angle is zero or parallel to the X axis. The result is shown below.

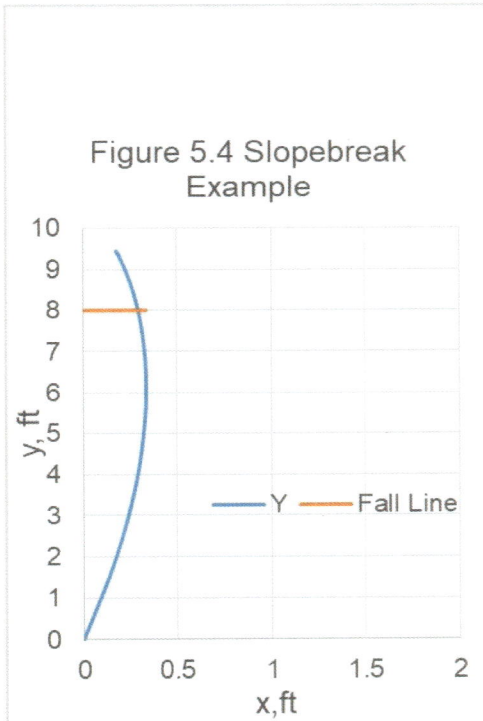

Figure 5.4 Slopebreak Example

Calculations for several values of Fall Line angles were conducted using the Golfpath © computer software. The first two results are for slope directions of ±10 degrees from the x direction. Results are shown in Figure 5.5a,b. For a fall line of + 10 degrees there is more effect of gravity slowing the ball down so it falls short at y = 8.8 ft. For a fall line of -10 degrees gravity helps speed up the ball and it goes beyond the hole at y = 10.5 ft.

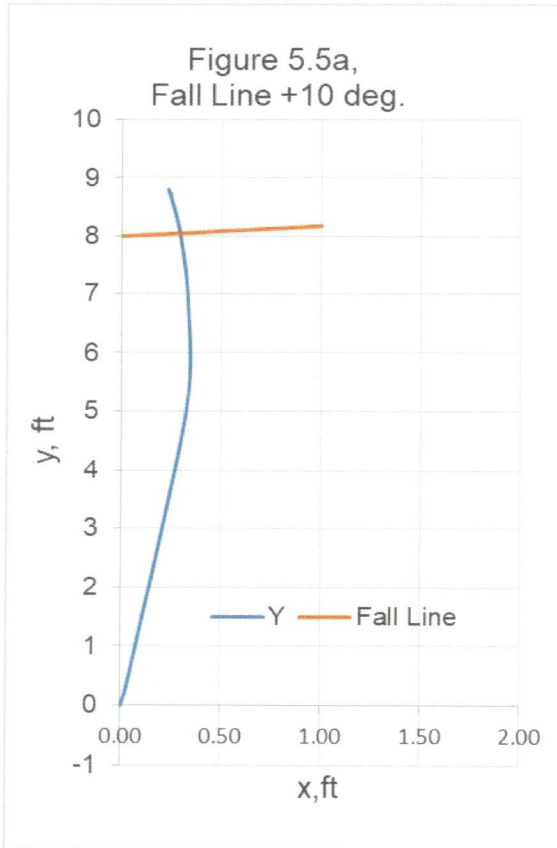

Figure 5.5a,
Fall Line +10 deg.

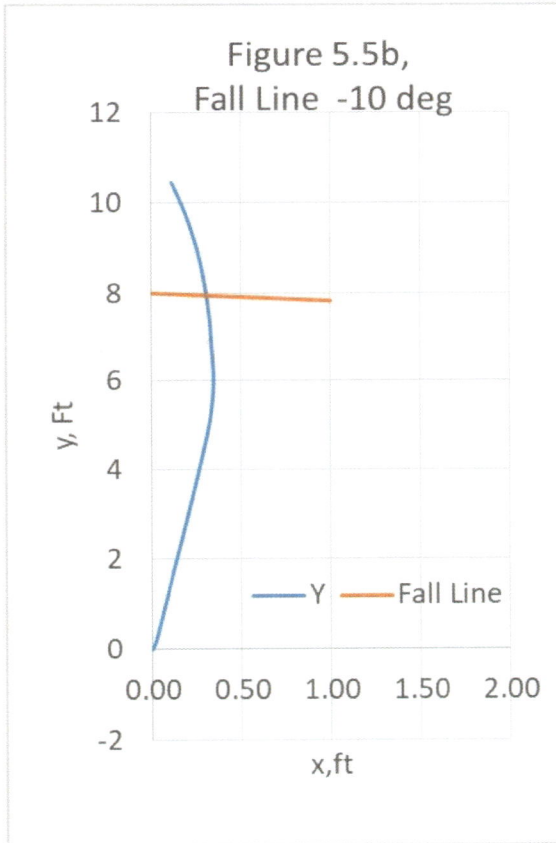

Figure 5.5b, Fall Line -10 deg

Conclusion: A very small change in orientation of the fall line can cause the putt to miss the hole by several inches.

Next consider the case if the fall line is oriented at − 30 degrees. We expect some help from gravity so we try a lower velocity at Vo = 5.5 fps. The result from the GOLFPATH analysis is shown in Figure 5.6.

Figure 5.6 Slopebreak Example
psi = -30 deg., Vo = 5.5 fps

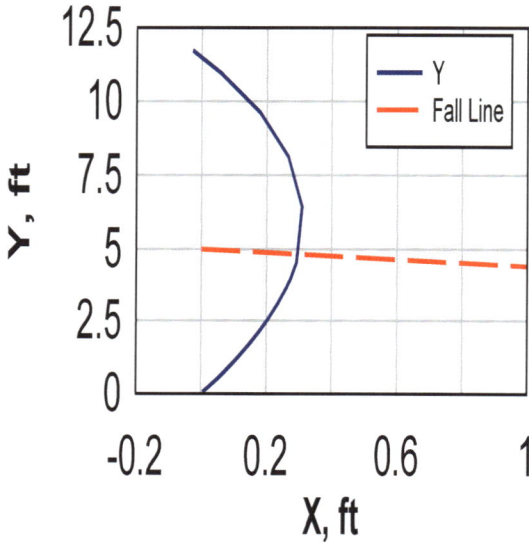

The ball over shot the hole to y = 11.7 ft but it reached the X = 0 axis. Because of the "similarity of paths" if we reduce the velocity still further we will still reach the X =0 axis.. Let us use the Master Chart, the first chart on in Chapter 1. The X coordinate is replaced by the Y coordinate since we are now putting in the Y direction.

The chart with the Y coordinate is reprinted below. For Yr =

11.7 ft and Y to the hole Yh = 10 ft, we have Yr/Yh = 1.17.
This is close to 1.2 and from the chart we try Vh/Vr = 0.91.

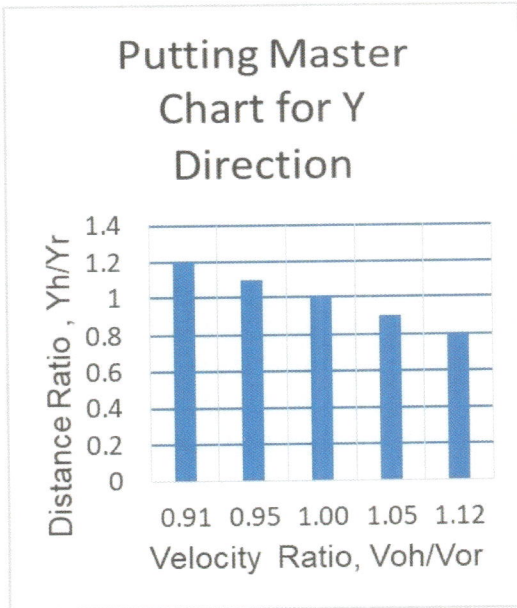

So we reduce the velocity by about 10 % from 5.5 to 5.0
fps. The result from the GOLFPATH analysis is shown in
Figure 5.6a.

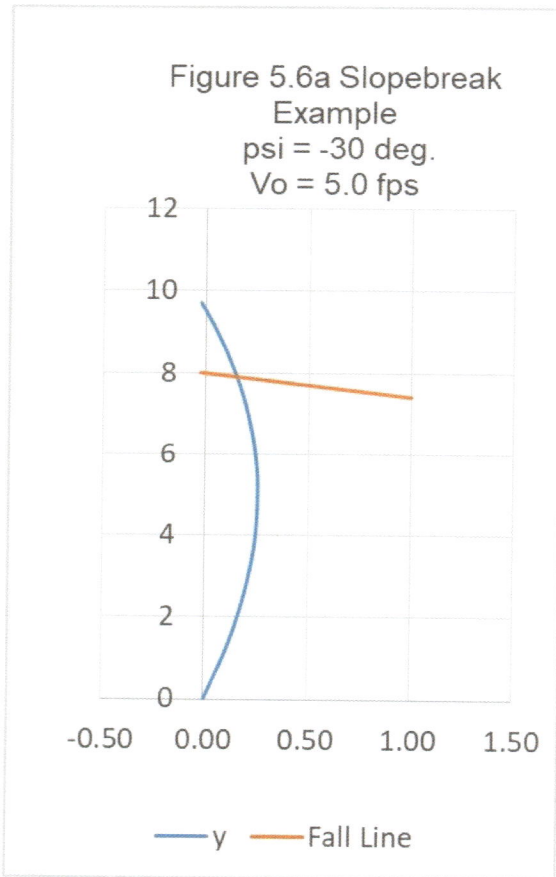

Figure 5.6a Slopebreak Example
psi = -30 deg.
Vo = 5.0 fps

It is evident the ball comes close to y = 10 ft and the master chart works also for the sloping green with a Fall Line at – 30 degrees. This is because of the similarity of paths with the same target line at X = 1 ft as described in Chapter 2 above.

The next case is for a slope the opposite way with the fall line at +30 degrees. A larger velocity should be used because gravity is now opposing the Y component of the velocity. With the putting velocity of 6.5 fps and with the same target xh of 1.0 ft it is found that the ball misses to the right as shown in Figure 5.6b.

Figure 5.6b
Slopebreak Example
psi = +30 deg.
Vo = 6.5 fps

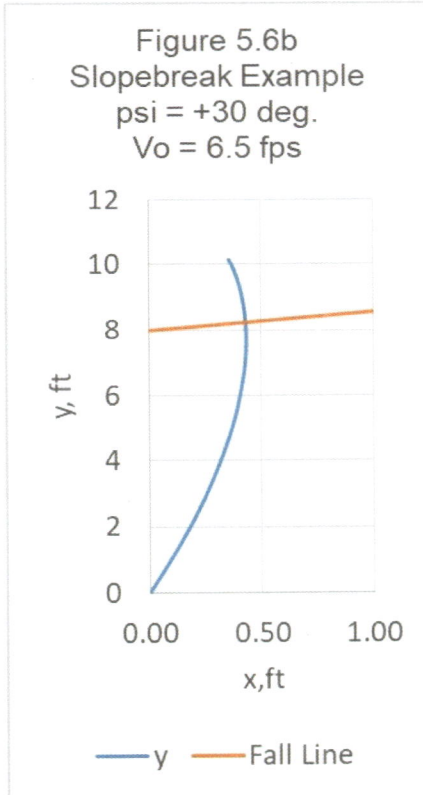

Next the target must be shifted to the left. From the above curve we see that the ball reaches Y = 10 ft at a value of x about 0.4 ft. for Vo = 6.5 fps. So we change our target to Xh = 1.0 - .4 = 0.6 ft, about 7 inches.

It is found that the ball comes close to the hole a shown in Figure 5.6c.

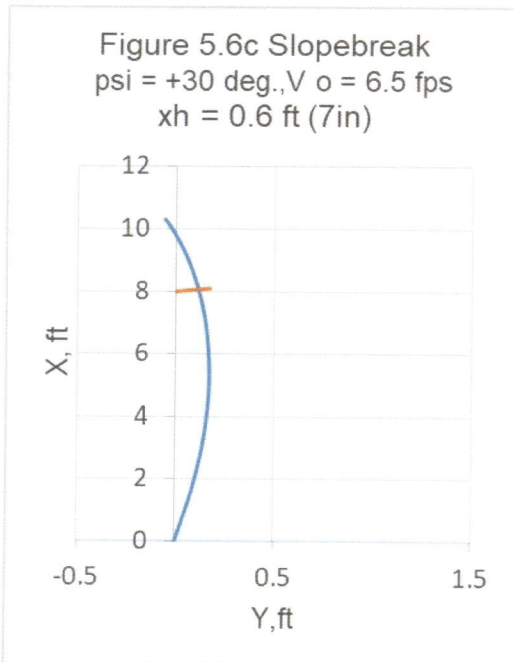

Figure 5.6c Slopebreak
psi = +30 deg.,V o = 6.5 fps
xh = 0.6 ft (7in)

What if the hole is located at 12 ft instead of 10 ft? Using the Master Chart we estimate a velocity of about 10% more or about 1.1 * 6.5 or 7.15. Let us try Vo = 7 fps. The result is shown below. The ball just about reaches the hole.

Again the master chart works also for the sloping green with a Fall Line at + 30 degrees. This is because of the similarity of paths described in Chapter 2 but now with the same target line at at X = 7 inches.

Figure 5.6d. Slopebreak Example
psi = +30 deg., Vo = 7 fps
Xh = 0.6 ft (7 in)

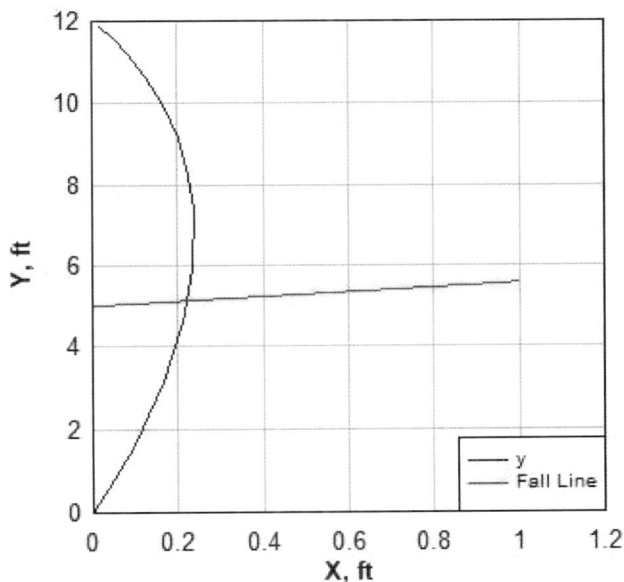

The above examples show how important it is to estimate the target Break Point distance xh and the Fall Line angle. However the master chart helps a lot because we do not need to know exactly what the Fall Line angle is. A practice putt or a previous putt serves as an input to the Master Chart that determines what velocity the next stroke should be.

The GOLPATH software can be used to generate charts for other target values as well. For example is the chart below for a 2.5 degree slope (4.35 %), small resistance and Fall Line at zero. (Green with Stimpmeter reading of 13 ft)

Chart for Target Xh
2.5 degree slope, small resistance.
Fall Line, psi =0
Angle Φo,

deg		Xh/Yh	Xh/Vo^2	Yh/Vo^2
	76	0.135	0.048	0.358

Yh,ft		Xh,ft	Vo. fps
	8	1.08	4.73
	10	1.35	5.29
	12	1.62	5.79
	14	1.89	6.25

4 GOLF BALL PUTTING ANALYTICS

More results and details of the analysis may be found in the book, **GOLF BALL PUTTING ANALYTICS,** available at Amazon.com and Createspace.com. The Table of Contents of the book is given below.

Table of Contents of the book "GOLF BALL PUTTING ANALYTICS"

Appendix 1   GOLFPATH © - Predicting the Path of
Putting a Golf Ball on Sloping Greens, 2012
Appendix 2   Putting Straight Uphill or Straight Downhill
Appendix 3   Chipping and Pitching Onto the Green
Appendix 4   Chipping with Bouncing

ABOUT THE AUTHOR

Biographical Sketch

James C. Gerdeen, Professor Emeritus, UCD, University
of Colorado at Denver
Distinguished Professor, Michigan Technological
University
Education
Michigan Technological University BSME
Ohio State University MSEM
Stanford University   Ph.D.EM
Assoc. Free Lutheran Seminary   MDiv
Professional Experience
Adjunct Faculty, MAE, Missouri Science & Technology
Univ., Rolla, MO 2008
Adjunct Faculty, Missouri State Univ., Springfield, MO
2005-2012
Prof. & Chair of M. E. Dept., University of Colorado at
Denver. 1989-2002
Professor of Engineering Mechanics, Michigan
Technological University. 1968-1989
Senior Research Engineer, Battelle Columbus
Laboratories, Columbus, Ohio 1959-1968
Affiliate staff, Faculty Commons, University of Missouri,
Columbia, MO 2006-2018

Proof

Made in the USA
Columbia, SC
06 March 2018